THE
Butterfly
BOOK

Ready to Fly

MELINDA ANGELINA RUTHERFORD

WESTBOW
PRESS®
A DIVISION OF THOMAS NELSON
& ZONDERVAN

WestBow Press books may be ordered through booksellers or by contacting:

WestBow Press
A Division of Thomas Nelson & Zondervan
1663 Liberty Drive
Bloomington, IN 47403
www.westbowpress.com
1 (866) 928-1240

ISBN: 978-1-5127-8456-5 (sc)
ISBN: 978-1-5127-8457-2 (e)

Library of Congress Control Number: 2017906440

Print information available on the last page.

WestBow Press rev. date: 05/10/2017

Ready to Fly

Realizing if we don't take the chance, we can't
ever expect to know if what God
already told us is truly the
direction we are supposed to travel.
Years in the making

to be prepared to say
onward, net the fear, we may

fall, but then again what if
laying on the ground isn't that safe either.
Yonder... See it? We can fly!

Butterfly

Be strong and courageous,
understanding His plan for you,
that in all things He has control.
This very day, this life, He fore knew.
Every second He holds
righteously in command.
Forever being the final destination, but
living in Him now, in this land.
YOU!

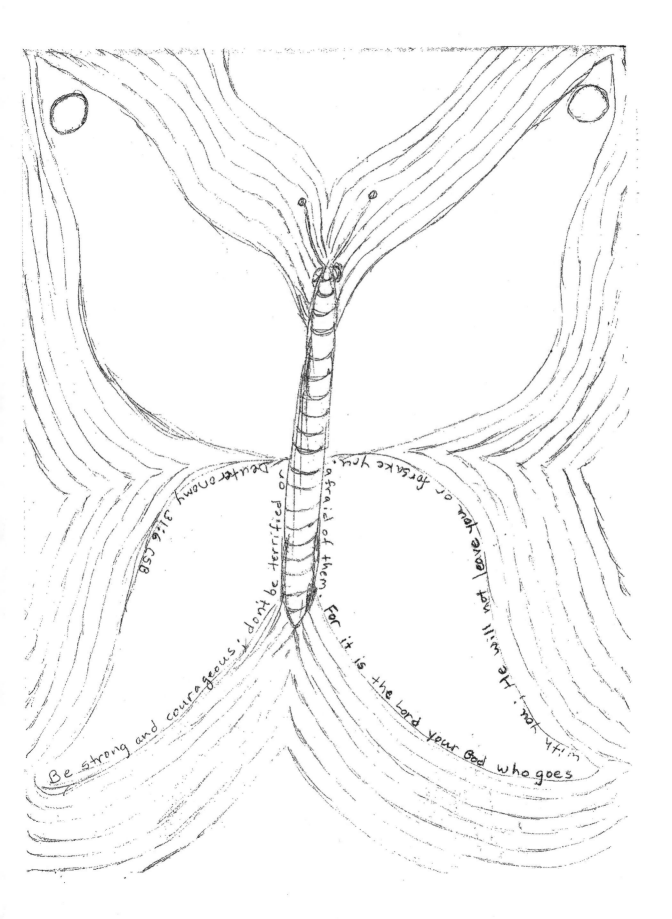

Be strong and courageous; don't be terrified or afraid of them. For it is the Lord your God who goes with him. He will not leave you or forsake you. Deuteronomy 31:6 CSB

Summer Azure

Shifty thinking
undoing what's presumably done.
My mind takes over
making me falter, the war's not won.
Eager for peace but
realizing there's nowhere to run.

Agonizing thoughts,
zealous to exercise in the son.
Ugly defiance,
recognizing, life, often, is not fun.
Exorcise the negative.

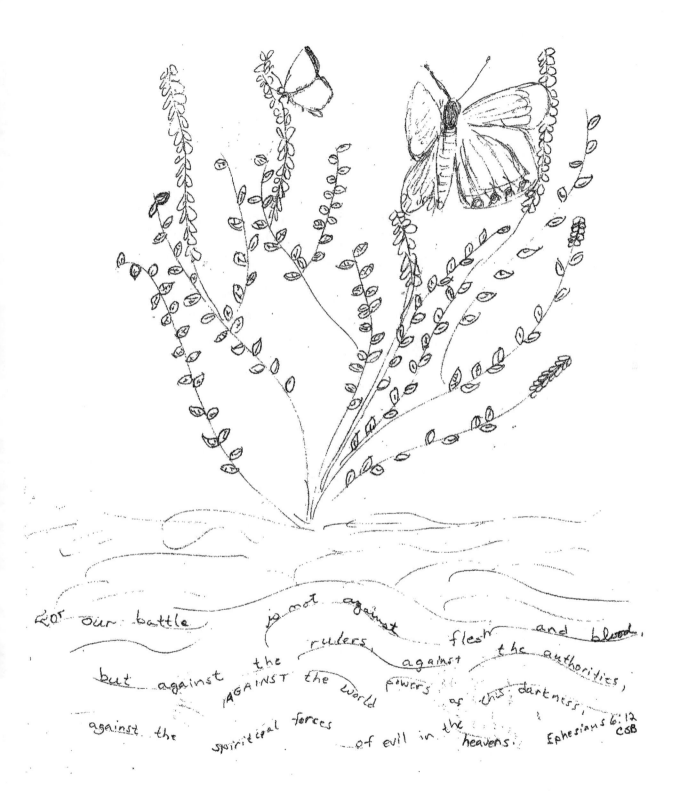

For our battle is not against flesh and blood, but against the rulers, against the authorities, AGAINST the world powers of this darkness, against the spiritual forces of evil in the heavens. Ephesians 6:12 CSB

5

Silvery Blue

Sleeping eludes me
in the darkness of night.
Leaving my dreams on the pillow
very envious of those who slumber.
Every hour ticks slowly on
reaching a point of no return.
You may as well just give in.

Be awake,
leave rest behind.
Use this silent time for
eternal things.

American Coppers

Almost making it here,
maybe I don't want to.
Easily forgotten ways of life,
really not easy at all.
Is this to be it?
Can the rest of earthly time
announce its end,
never home again?

Can space and time
oppress,
permitting some things,
passing on others?
Each day ticks on,
reaching the wicks end,
sunrise always sets.

...but our citizenship is in heaven Philippians 3:20 CSB

Bronze Coppers

Belonging,
really not.
On fast forward
now.
Zealous to just be
enjoying each moment.

Can space and time
oppress,
permitting some things,
passing on others?
Each day ticks on,
reaching the wicks end,
sunrise always sets.

THIS IS THE DAY THE LORD HAS MADE; LET US REJOICE AND BE GLAD IN IT.

PSALM 118:24

10

Bog Coppers

Belief, my anchor
Ongoing,
Giving me strength.

Can space and time
oppress,
permitting some things,
passing on others?
Each day ticks on,
reaching the wicks end,
sunrise always sets.

Silvery Checkerspot

Silliness is part of growing up,
isn't it?
Long after it's over, it leaves its mark.
Very deep pain, so hard to
explain, just say it, you'll feel
relieved. Problem is I can't say what I feel.
You want to help or maybe you don't.

Checking everywhere, everything.
Hearing noises that aren't there, fearing
everything because this world is a dangerous place.
Colored with sin, touching
kids in ways they should never
experience; stealing their silliness.
Reality is never really real again.
Shadows fill the mind and corners of the room.
Peace is hard to find.
Otherwise you might be taken by surprise, no
time for silliness, only a melted childhood.

Coral Hairstreak

Can I ever know
of the plans you have for me?
Really know?
Always searching,
leaving ideas in their infancy.

Hardly willing to try,
anxious about everything.
Inside me,
raging insecurity,
sincerely trying to hear.
Touch me please.
Reach out to me.
Eagerly waiting.
Already
knowing.

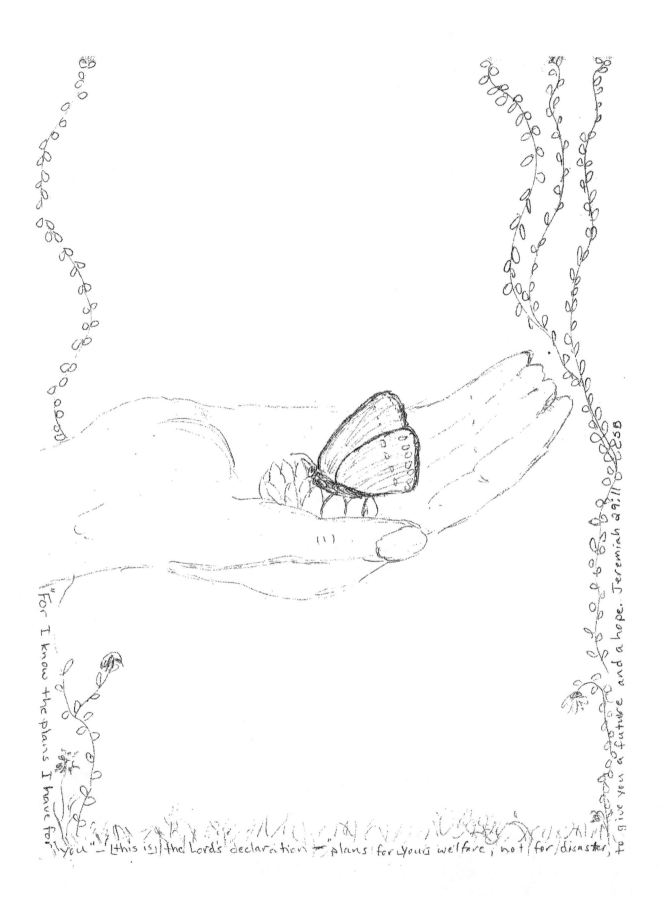

"For I know the plans I have for you" — [this is] the Lord's declaration — "plans for your welfare, not for disaster, to give you a future and a hope. Jeremiah 29.11 CSB

14

Early Hairstreak

Eager but
afraid.
Rarely believing the thoughts,
longing for some certainty.
Yearning for positive direction.

Hardly willing to try,
anxious about everything.
Inside me,
raging insecurity,
sincerely trying to hear.
Touch me please.
Reach out to me.
Eagerly waiting.
Already
knowing.

Gray Hairstreak

Gray skies weigh on my shoulders,
rain like memories that won't stop.
Anything can change
yet nothing does.

Hardly willing to try,
anxious about everything.
Inside me,
raging insecurity,
sincerely trying to hear.
Touch me please.
Reach out to me.
Eagerly waiting.
Already
knowing.

Eastern Pine Elfin

Easing into the Fall,
already gray hovers on our doorstep,
silently weighing down the hope
that wants to spring
eternal.
Realizing God does not always promise sunshine.
Nor does He promise absence of evil, not on this earth.

Promises of beauty, peace and love are
internally possible here but will
not abide in full until
eternity.

Easing into Fall with
love that cannot be bound by time or distance.
Figuring out how this struggle makes me more like Him.
Initiating control in the ways I can.
Never falling for what the world deems important.

Bog Elfin

Breaking through the darkness
on the brink of October,
glorious sunshine every day for so many.

Easing into Fall with
leaves that sprinkle the sky with color,
filling in to create a canvas immersed in beauty.
In every way amazing to behold,
never considering what is to come or what has passed,
just standing confidently in all His glory.

Consider the ravens: they don't sow or reap; they don't have a storeroom or a barn; yet God feeds them. Aren't you worth much more than the birds?

Luke 12:24 CSB

Eastern Tailed

Everything seems to hold promise.
All feels right, there is calm.
Suddenly life feels possible again, doable.
Tension has not disappeared,
even though it is harder to find,
ruling as it usually does but
not so, not right now.

Tally the days, maybe that's what I should do.
Always, may not really be.
It may just seem like "always" because
life feels so HARD when it is here.
Every sunny, better day is a blessing!
Don't ever forget to thank God! Thank you...

Baltimore

Believe
Admit
Love
Timeless
Ideas
Moving
Our
Reality toward
Eternity

If I take the wings of the morning, and dwell in the uttermost parts of the sea, Even there Your hand shall lead me, And Your right hand shall hold me. Psalm 139:9-10 NKJV

23

Question Mark

Quickly, seems to be the preset speed.
Unfortunately it is not mine.
Easing into each complicated situation
so I can fit in or at least appear to.
Troubling thoughts that I am not normal but
in fear I might just be like everyone else.
Only wanting to feel o k a y,
never minding if I'm cut from a different

mold but wishing at times I wasn't.
Are you real,
really, really there,
knowing and still loving.

Eastern Comma

East, West, North, South,
assuredly you are there.
Sitting on your throne,
though right here with me, everywhere.
Even in my sin you cared.
Righting my life gone terribly wrong.
Not in the program, but You still shared.

Constantly, totally, you did, you are, you will.
Only I wasn't and didn't but still
more son shone and warmed my nakedness.
More love flowed until I was bathed.
Awesomely you collected me and swayed.

Milbert's Tortoiseshell

Making it easier
Is not always the best answer.
Looking toward what promises
better days, weather, life
easily could just be a distraction.
Running, hoping, longing,
These can help us persevere but
so can they keep us from now.

This day holds its own life
or promises and hopes and dreams.
Running isn't always the only answer.
Take the time to figure
out what can I do here, now,
in this place. It will be
something different, maybe not feel as good.
Easy, probably not, but I'm pretty
sure there is something
here that would definitely be good
enough.
Love is here, quit trying so hard,
love is here, already.

Mourning Cloak

Mourning can mean sadness,
or a new beginning,
utter despair, fear or
realizing I am strong.
Never wanting it to end.
Internally aching.
Never to say
good-bye.

Can you see me through this?
Longing to feel
okay
again.
Knowing I will, I have to.

you by your name; You are Mine. When you pass through the waters, I will be with you; And through the rivers, they shall not overflow you. When you walk through the fire, you shall not be burned, Nor shall the flame scorch you. Isaiah 43:1b-2 NKJV

"Fear not, for I have redeemed you; I have called

28

Red Admiral

Realizing there is promise.
Each moment unfolds, a new surprise.
Days can be like this.

Almost
despondent but then
miraculously the Word
involving the truth of great love
readjusts the whole picture
and it makes sense again.
Love warms and encourages and lifts me up!

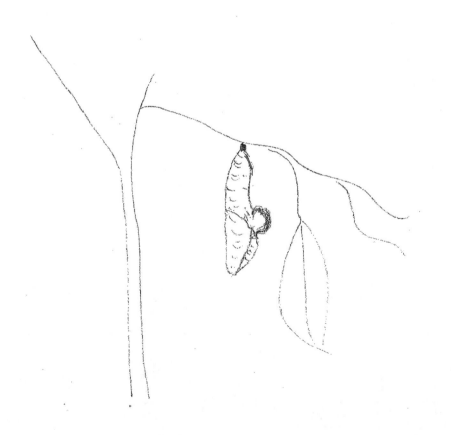

Common Buckeye

Can I be the encourager?
Only in truth but sharing the
message, you are loved. No
matter what has ever happened to you,
on this day know you are loved.
No One can take His care and regard from you!

Be cognizant, they will try.
Underdogs want you to drown with them.
Can you feel the warmth of the light?
Knowing, the light searches to fill you,
expecting you to do nothing.
You just need to accept the warmth.
Everything will be okay.

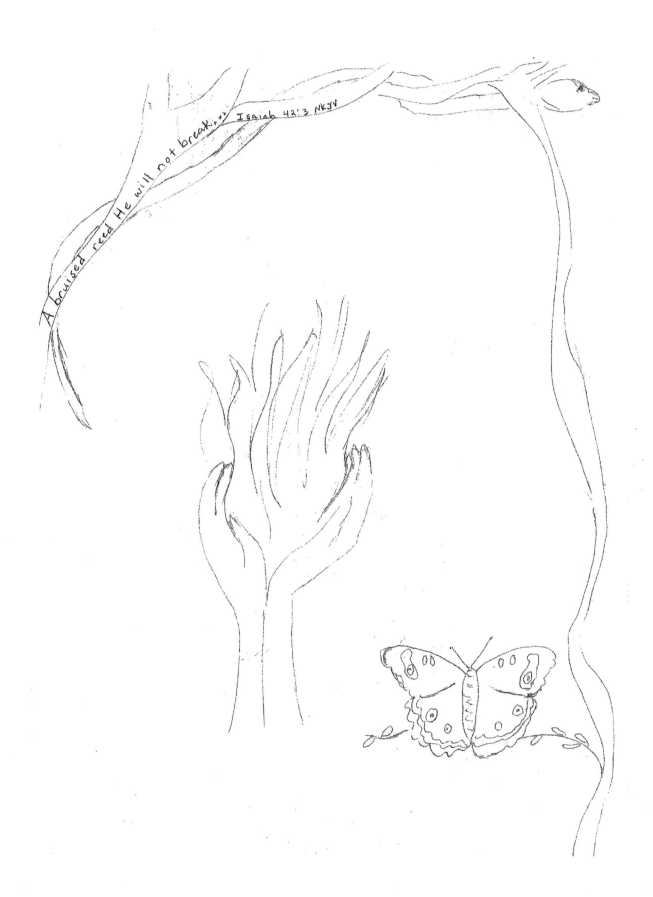

A bruised reed He will not break... Isaiah 42:3 NKJV

Red Spotted Admiral

*Round and round I go, there is no
end. I just start to feel
distance from discouragement.*

*Sunshine has even broken the black barrier.
Purposely exercising to help lift this dread,
only to sit alone with
tears hiding heavy and full,
threatening to fall in a torrent,
escaping with no way to
dam the flood.*

*Actually
depression just might be
my friend.
Intellectually I would never
realize this to be true or
admit I create the most when
left in my cavern of doubt.*

Why are you cast down, O my soul? And why are you disquieted within me? Hope in God, for I shall yet praise Him for the help of His countenance. Psalm 42:5 NKJV

Viceroy

Victorious
In spite of all that has been taken, you
can stand in strength with
energy that comes from being part of a
Royal family, an heir.
On your head the crown of glory.
You are Victorious!

Little Wood Satyr

Little did I know 5 years ago
in the midst of a busy, purposeful life
that I would be here in this place?
The place itself is not bad,
like being on a long vacation,
every nook and cranny filled with nature.

Woods and wildlife just outside my window.
On good days it feels like paradise.
On bad days the forest closes in with a
dread so real it beckons me, come.

So much of life can be wasted,
and to what purpose?
To show you, little you, control me.
You do not control me or anything,
really, unless we let you, we have to let you.

37

Common Wood Nymph

Can the state
of
my
mind really keep me
on course or off?
Now, today, this second?

Would you allow
ongoing torment,
ongoing
doubt?

Not that I have no part but
you, you are the
Magnificent One, owner, creator High
Priest of all.
How do I figure this out?

Queen

Questioning is good,
unless
endless questions absorb the
energy needed to take the first step.
Now! Your time is now!

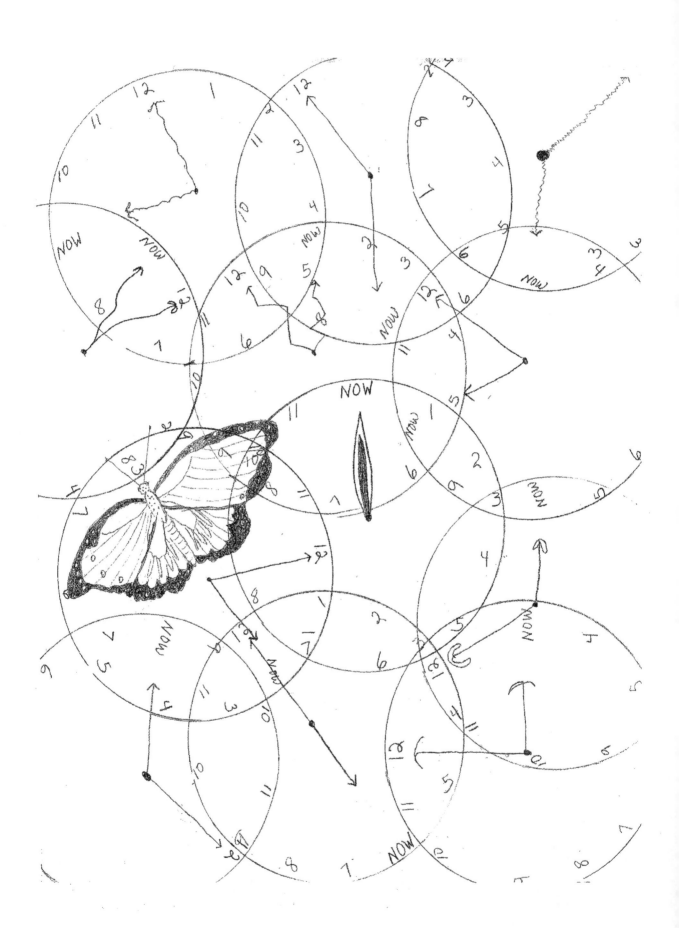

Soldier

So my love, you have decided
on a path of purpose that
lets you be in
danger, and maybe though scary,
it is a path I admire.
Even as a toddler harm was
real for you, God will keep you safe.

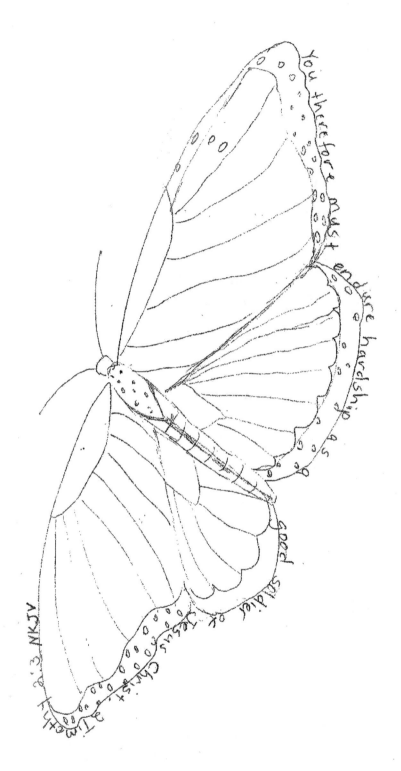

You therefore must endure hardship as a good soldier of Jesus Christ. Timothy 2:3 NKJV

Tiger Mimic Queen

The calendar implies it is summer.
I gaze from my window wondering.
Gray skies abound, it seems like
everlasting torture,
revealing the pettiness of my complaint.

Many in this world suffer
in ways unimaginable,
more ways than we want to admit.
Ignore, deflect, keep busy.
Can we, so little, make a difference?

Question the status quo – start here.
Usher in new understanding,
energize the troops, accumulate resources.
Every person counts, every single soul.
Never ever forget, you too are loved!

brass or a clanging symbol. 2 And though I have the gift of prophecy, not love, it profits me nothing. 4 Love suffers long and is kind; love all things, hopes all things, endures all things. 8a Love

and understand all mysteries and all knowledge, and though I have all faith, so that I could re- love never fails. 1 Corinthians 13:1-8a NKJV does not envy; love does not parade itself, is not puffed up; 5 does not behave rudely,

Though I speak with the tongues of men and of angels, but have not love, I have become sounding bestow all my goods to feed the poor, and though I give my body to be burned, but have does not rejoice in iniquity, but rejoices in the truth; 7 bears all things, believes

move mountains, but have not love, I am nothing. 3 And though I does not seek its own, is not provoked, thinks no evil; 6

God is love

44

Monarch

Mankind has forgotten the
Only true source of life.
Nourishing sick ideas of importance
And entertainment.
Reality, a show on TV.
Come on, wake up, we
Have only one true King!

Guava Skipper

Giving way for your majesty *to appear.*
Understanding there is more than one path
Allowing us to fulfill your calling.
Verifying finally is this it?
Allowing my faith to overwhelm my fear.

Seeking comfort with
Knowledge.
It will never be
Perfect here.
Perhaps you can glimpse
Eternity and
Realize it is for you.

Mangrove Skipper

Men have the power to hurt us,
And we have the power together to say
No more! This must stop, this
Gross injustice and destruction of life.
Righteous anger belongs to us
Only to be treated like yesterday's trash.
Vastly ignored, unheard, defamed,
Everlasting love is hard to conceive.

Hatred stirs up strife, but love covers all sins. Proverbs 10:12 NKJV

49

Hammock Skipper

Having to work hard to believe
And or accept what my gift may be.
Making an effort to test it out,
Maybe I will finally see.
Others have such special gifts
Clearly sent from thee.
Knowing hard work is needed, perhaps the missing piece?

Christina's Sulphur

*Coming
here was a process,
rightly so.
Inching your way with
strength and
trepidation
into our waiting arms.
Not sure if you could trust,
aware,
so many have let you down.*

*Strength, maybe a façade?
Until you tried and you've
learned through hard work and
pain that it may not be easy
here, but you are strong.
Ultimately in charge, marching on to
realize your dreams.*

Yet in all these things we are   more than conquerors through Him who

loved u.s. Romans 8:39 NKJV

53

Pink Edged

Please help me
in this pursuit,
not really
knowing why

energy is put into
doing silly,
godless things.
Even me, wanting purpose but
devoted to my own pleasure.

Queen Alexandra's

Quickly asserting that
under the circumstances
each distraction tempts me to
entertain the idea that
now is not the time to create.

After all there are toilets to clean,
laundry to fold and put away,
edging, weeding, mowing mulching.
Xavier study (the Saint not the aptitude test)
and an endless list of things
not really needing immediate attention
determined to
render me
a life of repetitive motion that
steals the real calling hidden in me, in us...

Scudders

Seriously where is all this darkness
coming from? My husband
uttered my writing fills him with
dread, thinking he should return to bed.
Don't believe I'm unhappy, blessings are
endless in my life I
realize this and am so grateful. Just
sometimes...the world feels sad.

Meads

My skin, so hot from the bright sun,
enjoying every heated moment,
and ignoring the truth:
Dark days will come, trying to
smother the life springing in me!

Canadian

Can't believe how many years have passed
and you are still gone.
Nothing replaces actually seeing your face.
All the memories, good and bad, remain.
Dying doesn't take you from my heart .
In many things you will always be
a perfect piece of a life in me, but for
now, I just wish I could hold you one more time.

Written August 5, 2014

Johansens

Justifying the feeling
only serves to a reason why,
hastening my own believing
and prolonging the urge to fly.
No one has ever asked the story,
so the truth may not be told.
Endless recollections flooding,
never ending secret, always mine to hold.
Seemingly unscathed but obvious cracks in the mold.

Dainty Sulpher

Dare to dream, to believe
and work toward the finished product.
Instill necessary steps to make it happen,
not thoughts crowding in, even now.
Thoughts saying
you will never amount to anything.

So you hear the user and deny the creator,
until God's voice, love, becomes more real,
linked to every neuron of your troubled mind.
Phony realities belonging to the evil one
have prominence, they stomp the
unusual but prolific beauty of the
real you.

Two Barred Flasher

Thunder cracking with a vengeance,
waiting briefly then exploding,
only to prove its power.

Breaking the silence
and propelling the rain.
Rolling in without warning.
Rolling out again.
Energy released ever
daunting in its magnitude.

Flashing light across the sky,
limited only by the
Almighty, playing games with my mind.
Sunshine once again evades us
here in the midst of summer.
Every day hopeful but
reality has left me behind.

Small spotted

Situated on a little hill.
Many came to watch.
Alluring, the ugliness
languishing by choice,
loving without hesitance.

So, so
perfect are You and
only You
that being like you is
the thing that challenges in
every way imaginable and
directs me to my own ugliness.

Frosted Flasher

Forever useful, is that what you once thought?
Rotting here totally covered
over by foliage and wild flowers.
Standing firm but with no chance of revival.
Traveling was once your core purpose.
Ending up here like this never crossed your mind.
Deciding your fate, a culture of technology.

Forgetting the importance you once held,
longing for progress but realizing some of the
allure of prosperity dims the importance, ignores
symptoms unraveling right before your eyes.
How do we not see the pain
evolving in what once was family? In
reality you are beautiful just the way you are.

Gilbert's

Glory be to God, everyday,
in every way, praise His name.
Leasing your creation
because it is Yours, never ours
emotes a flush of gratitude.
Realizing it is for our pleasure,
that taking care of it is
something we must treasure.

Desert Orangetip

Don't believe there is a day more beautiful anywhere on this
earth, than this day, right now and right here.
Ships are sailing, making their way out to sea.
Ethereal, the leaves as they gently rustle in the cool breeze.
Reaching the deepest fibers of my being with
that beauty that can only be explained by intelligent design.

Ornately scattered flowers and well-trodden paths.
Requirement is to only enjoy, be present
and
never, ever forget to be thankful,
grateful for
everything we have.
Thinking of how blessed I am only reminds me of
injustice and those who are in need, a
powerful reminder that there is much work to do.

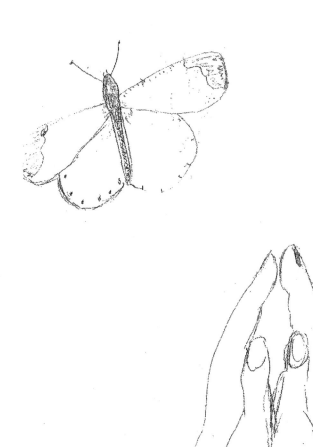

Purpose

Falcate Orangetip

Falling slowly into darkness,
although you seemed okay.
Loving, though hard at times,
can be a labor all in itself.
Always trying to do right,
trying to be right,
enjoying the simple things.

Overlooked and underpaid,
rarely asking for anything.
Although you did have your desires,
nothing ever came before family.
Getting up in those dark years,
even that was for us.
Thank-you for what you could do,
instilling a love that did not diminish but
probably grew with time, no matter what.
Written August 21, 2014

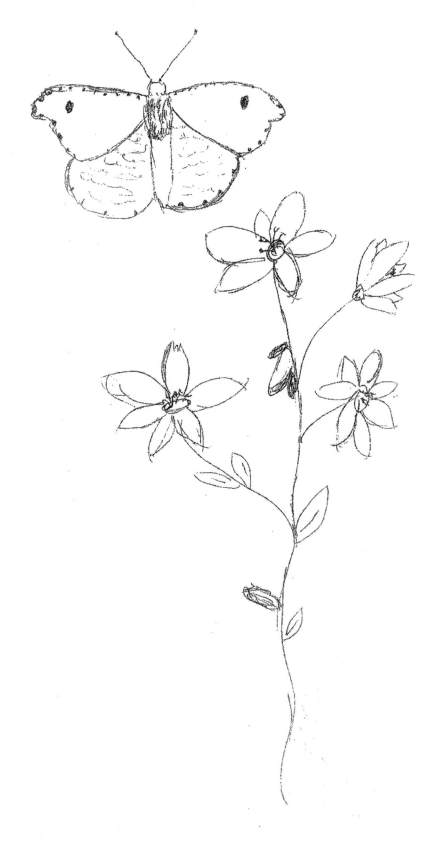

Eastern Tiger (Swallowtails)

Even though it may seem like
all I ever think is negative,
sort of like a broken record,
that never really
ever played a happy song.
Really the truth is there has
never been a time I didn't feel grateful.

The real truth
is, in all my darkness
God continues to shed light, and I
enjoy the beauty everyday in some way.
Rarely is a time there is not at least a glimmer.

Spicebush Swallowtail
Somehow I knew.
Perhaps it was the stillness
in spite of recent activity
causing alarm.
Eagerly searching for the
babies who
usually made little
squawking noises
however small to call for their parents.
Something happened though.
When? I don't know for sure,
although it must have been recent.

Loving parents fought for you.
Loving parents tried to ward
off the evil, the bigger, stronger
will of
those who plunder
and bring shame on all called human.
I don't understand this atrocity but
love doesn't always flow from me either.
Pipevine

Possibly I would have been EMO
in high school. I mean
perhaps just weird.
Everyone seemed so different than me,
varying degrees of normal
in a colorless culture.
Never really understanding,
every day crawling deeper inside.

Anise Swallowtail

And
Now
I
See
Easily.

Sanity was in question.
Wanting to be the same
and concern that
laughing at me,
looking at me
oddly
was my fault, inherently.
The idea that
all the meanness was
inside them, never occurred to me.
Laughing to cover their own fear, pain.

Fear not, for I am with you, Be not dismayed, for I am your God. I will strengthen you, Yes, I will help you, I will uphold you with My righteous right hand. Isaiah 41:10 NKJV

Giant

Growing, playing, having fun.
In an instant the world changes.
Always laughing enjoying the sun,
not suspecting.
Tragedy, the end of you.

Ornythion Swallowtail

Only God gives the
right answer all the time.
No one else is omniscient.
You, in your relationship,
trust what
He says to you!
It is as important and
on spot as what any other has to say.
No one is your god except God.

Search His
Word
always,
listening with a heart of
love and with an
open mind.
Waiting for Him
to
answer because He always does, He
Is speaking to you
loud and clear.

White - Dotted Cattleheart

Women,
how did
it happen
that it is generally accepted
each of us are the same?

Does it make sense
on any realm
to say we, created in His image
that we, who by His blood
each are made like the other?
Dying he loosed the curtain.
Certainly our gifts
are accepted for they are from His hand.
The ones
that seem questionable to some
leave me with furrowed brow.
Earth
Heaven
Everywhere
All are one in Christ,
Right?
Then make it so!

Bahamian

Before today I
always
had the idea that writing
and
making a book was
in some way only for someone else.
All this time it's how You speak to me
now that is really something

Printed in the United States
By Bookmasters